This book belongs to

_____

For all parents who want their children to learn different cultures and traditions.

Special thanks to my friends - Asim, Farzia and Tasneem for helping me write this book. To each one of you, I am grateful.

Ramadan
my first fast

Meet our friend Ali, who is very eager to start his Ramadan fast. But he is too young to fast from dawn to dusk.

After a LOT of pleading, Ali convinced his Mom to allow him to fast for a day and Ali is very excited.

I jump up high,
with excitement and joy.
It is my FIRST Ramadan fast,
and I can't wait to start.

I see the moon,
shining brightly in the sky.
It's more vibrant than ever,
I ask why?

The Ramadan month
starts with the sighting
of the crescent moon

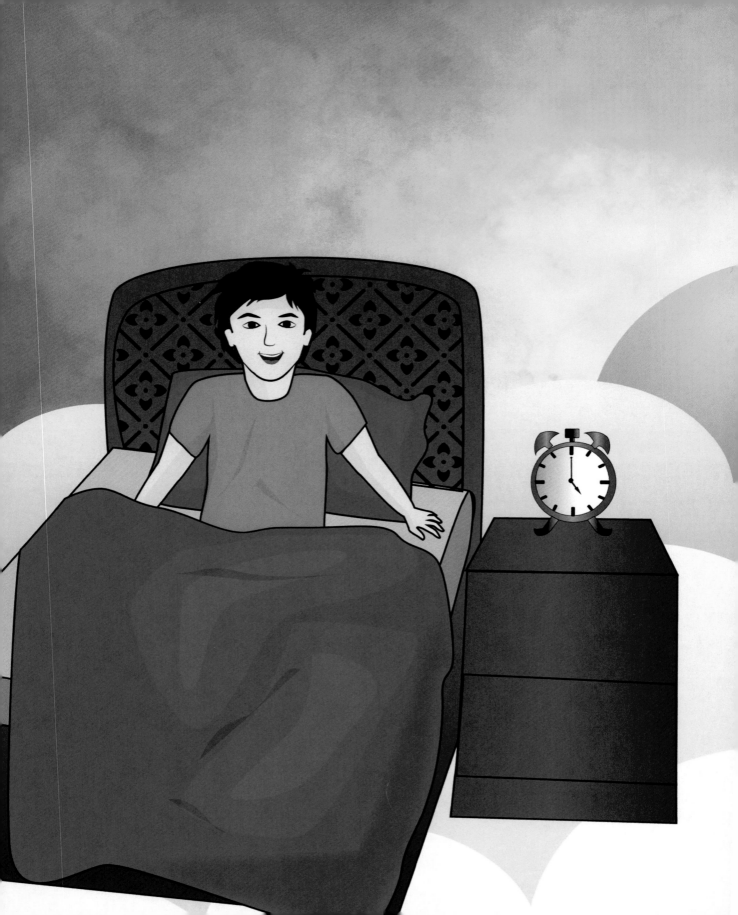

It is time for Suhoor,
so I wake up early at five.
I plan to stuff my belly,
before the sunrise.

Suhoor is the
pre-dawn meal consumed
before fasting.

Mom filled my plate
with extra bread.
Reminded me once again,
no food or water until sunset.

I went about my day
the usual way,
Meeting friends
as I sway and play.

By the afternoon
I felt the hunger pangs.
All I could think of
were pizzas, donuts, and strawberry jams.

I asked my brother,
"Doesn't your stomach
grumble and rumble?"

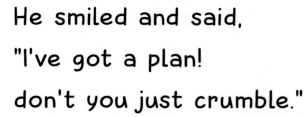

He smiled and said,
"I've got a plan!
don't you just crumble."

So then we both read
verses from the Quran.
Magically, my hunger vanished
in a short span.

The Quran is the
holy book of Islam.

Soon, we heard the
evening Adhan.
This meant
the sun was down.

The Adhan is the evening call to prayer.

We broke our fast with sweet dates,
and sumptuous dishes as we loaded our plates.

Mom and Dad congratulated me
on my first fast.

They showered me with presents -
a board game and a brown hat.

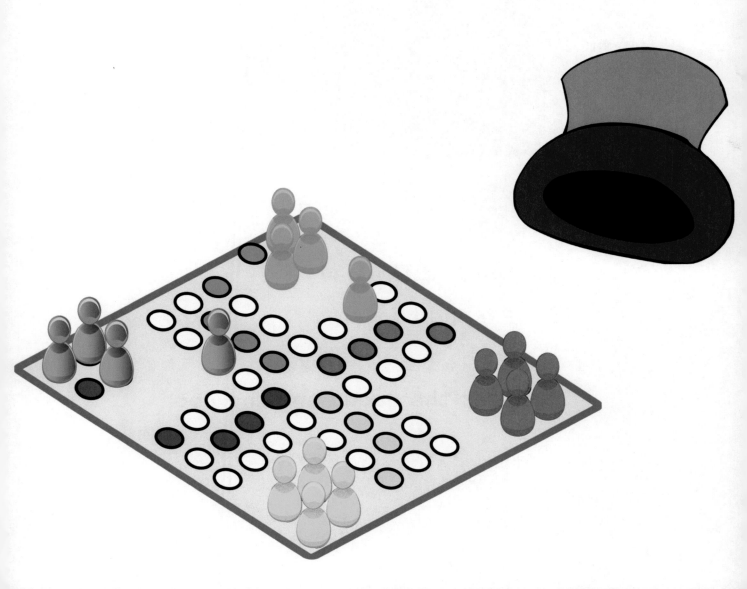

As I passed the day
in pain and hunger,
It taught me empathy
towards the needy and the poor.

I used my savings to donate some gifts.
With this act of kindness, I experienced joy and happiness.

Today is Eid-al-fitr,
the day of rejoice and celebration.
We offered our special Eid prayers
with faith and devotion.

Eid-al-fitr is a festival that marks the end of Ramadan.

We spent the day
greeting relatives and friends.
Eid-al-fitr is celebrated
after the Ramadan month ends.

THE HOLY MONTH OF RAMADAN

During the month of Ramadan, the Prophet Mohammed received the first revelations of the Quran. As a mark of gratitude and respect for the guidance received from God, this month is observed by all Muslims as the holy month. Fasting during Ramadan is also one of the five pillars of Islam.

People pass this month in prayers, fasting, and charitable activities.

About the author

Anitha Rathod

Anitha Rathod was born in the historic city of Hyderabad, India. She studied Finance and Human Resources from the Indian Institute of Management, Lucknow, and worked with corporates for more than 9 years before deciding to pursue her passion for writing and creating books. She is the mother of two young and naughty kids.

This book is a part of the festival series. Every festival comes with a legend and history of its own. Through these books, we can learn to stay connected to our roots and traditions.

If you like the book, please post your review on

https://www.amazon.com/Ramadan-First-Fast-Unravel-Festivals/

dp/1798719258/

www.anitharathod.com

Eid
Mubarak

Made in the USA
Middletown, DE
22 April 2019